AF129974

Contents

How to Use This Deck

Welcome to a new beginning. This deck contains exercises that can be used to reflect, grow, and develop healthy connections, with the ultimate goal of improving your self-esteem. Be encouraged to review this booklet first, as it will provide insights into the basics of self-esteem, how it impacts our lives, and what gets in the way of a healthy sense of self-esteem. You'll also receive tips on how to create healthy new habits to maintain the sense of self you may be longing for.

The accompanying deck is divided into six categories: Self-Awareness, Self-Acceptance, Self-Assertiveness, Self-Esteem and Purpose, Self-Esteem and Core Beliefs, and Self-Esteem and Boundaries. Start wherever you wish—there is no right or wrong way to proceed, and each card can be selected at random. Move at your own pace when engaging in the activities, and please know there is no pressure to complete the deck within 100 days. Instead, focus on staying committed to yourself and your goals during this time of self-exploration.

What Is Self-Esteem?

In simple terms, self-esteem is the value and worth we hold in ourselves. Self-esteem is a trait, a state, and a need, influenced by both nature and nurture. Let's explore how.

Our view of self is influenced by our relationships, experiences, personal beliefs, and environments. It's easy to believe that our self-esteem, whether positive or negative, remains the same over time and defines who we are. But this is not true. Self-esteem is not fixed; it can change over time. Consider how you felt about yourself as a child and how that view of yourself may have changed as you became an adult. Perhaps as a child, you exuded confidence until you experienced the heartache of negative messaging from someone you trusted. In adulthood, you might have encountered moments of success yet struggle to believe you are worthy of the accolades you receive. This is a hint of imposter syndrome, a heightened sense of low self-esteem.

Self-esteem can be impacted by several other factors, including our cultural and religious background, mental health, and trauma. Understandably, having a mental health diagnosis such as depression or social anxiety impacts not only how we see the world but also how we view ourselves in the world. Self-esteem is also impacted by our social connections. Consider this: Does your self-esteem change depending on whom you're talking to? Do you ever notice how your self-esteem plummets when you are in a bad relationship?

All of these factors can play into the self-esteem we have, and the level of self-esteem can range from minimal or nonexistent to a healthy high that allows us to believe in ourselves and our capabilities, regardless of what others (or society) may say, do, or believe.

Be encouraged that improving your self-esteem is a journey. It takes time, and you deserve to make yourself a priority. Take a moment to recognize that you have entered a space to improve your self-esteem and, in addition, to recognize and embrace who you truly are at the core. The time you invest in yourself with this self-esteem deck can pay off in ways you have yet to imagine. It is my hope that the transformation of your mindset will lead to greater self-awareness, improved relationships, and a new, brighter out-look on who you are and the possibilities ahead.

The Basics of Self-Esteem

Do you know how special you are? This question might be difficult to answer. Before you allow your thoughts to carry you to a place of despair, let me tell you that you are more than special—you are extraordinary. How can I say this? Well, the truth is that we are all extraordinary. We are each unique— there is nobody exactly like us, and we contain distinctive thoughts, perspectives, and gifts that are solely ours. We are each capable of changing the world.

You may feel alone in your struggle with self-esteem. And when we feel discouraged and self-critical, our instincts may urge us to hide from the world. It's important to know you are not alone. It is estimated that a staggering 85 percent of people struggle with low self-esteem.

As you learn to accept yourself, my hope is that you find new ways to love yourself exactly as you are. The change we want to see in the world starts from within. And as you work on this goal, you may find that connecting with others and sharing your experiences can foster healing for you as well as others in your life who feel similarly.

Self-Esteem as a Need

According to Maslow's hierarchy of needs, self-esteem is a basic need that all humans possess—it's just as important as our need for food, clothing, shelter, safety, and connection. Self-esteem impacts our ability to experience life fully or at our highest potential. A lack of self-esteem affects every part of our existence, from work performance to relationships to physical and mental health. It can cause us to believe the lie that we are unworthy of love and belonging.

Now, don't get discouraged if your work performance, relationships, or feelings of well-ness are not ideal at this moment. As you work through this deck and focus on improving your self-esteem, you will likely notice opportunities to show up, care for yourself, and connect with others in a new way, further fostering your sense of value and belonging. To operate at your best—emotionally, mentally, and physically—requires a healthy sense of self-esteem. Find peace in know-ing you're exactly where you need to be to begin meeting your need for positive self-esteem.

Prepare for the Work

Your decision to improve your self-esteem is not a coincidence. This is a purposeful moment in time, stemming from a choice you made to actualize your best future self.

As you read this, take a moment to think about how you feel in this moment. Are you excited? Ready? Nervous? Unsure about the timing? It's okay. All of these feelings are natural. Let me be the first to congratulate you on taking action toward the change you seek. You *are* ready, and now *is* the time!

As you proceed through the exercises in this deck, be gentle with yourself. Take things slowly and be mindful of how you're feeling along the way. There may be times when you feel over-whelmed by the moments of reflection in these exercises. You might recognize that a fear of looking deeply within yourself has blocked you from becoming your best self. So, before you even select your first card, start by taking time to establish your goals and consider your "why." Ask yourself, *Why do I want to improve my self-esteem* and *Why now? What is my motivation?*

Your self-esteem reflects your internalized experiences and beliefs about ourselves, but the journey to improving your self-esteem need not be taken alone. Throughout this deck, you'll be encouraged to practice various skills with someone you trust. Consider whom you feel comfortable with to support you in your growth.

Finally, be patient with yourself, and remember that change does not happen overnight. Take this time to visualize yourself accomplishing your goals and living your best life—each small step will bring you closer to becoming the best version of yourself you've always imagined.

Materials

The exercises in this deck don't require much, if anything. Some activities will invite you to use a journal. Take this time to start a new journal or notebook and use your favorite pen or pencil. If you prefer to use an audio journal, just ensure that you have space on your cell phone or tablet to save voice notes. Some exercises involve the use of the internet or your phone's camera, and a few others invite you to create with poster paper, printouts, scissors, glue, and markers. Lastly, you may find it helpful to establish a quiet, comfortable place where you won't be distracted or disturbed to complete the activities.

How to Build Habits

When we are working toward change, consistency and repetition are key to creating and maintaining a new way of being. To expedite this, consider selecting one card the same time every day or the same day every week. Reflection is another important practice during any journey of healing and growth. Set aside time to continue evaluating your goals for improving your self-esteem and considering your "why."

Choose a time and space that allows you to engage in the activities without distractions. This may require you to establish boundaries for yourself and with others to protect this time (we'll work on that together in this deck). Make time for rest and renewal. If you feel overwhelmed or struggle with thoughts of abandoning the process, understand that such feelings are normal with change. Be mindful of when these moments occur, as they may offer clues into the kinds of issues you resist. Most of all, make the decision now that if these moments arise, you will always choose to persevere. You are stronger than you know.

Common Internal Blocks

During the process of working toward change, it's common to experience internal blocks. This can feel confusing, especially when we feel strongly that we are ready for change. You don't need to accept these moments as defeat, but rather view them as checkpoints in the process that you can work past with a few valuable strategies. Here are a few common internal blocks you may experience as you engage in the exercises and some tips for getting past them.

SELF-SABOTAGE
We are often our worst enemies, biggest critics, and greatest barriers to long-lasting change. Self-sabotage occurs when we do things to intentionally prevent ourselves from success (even if we don't realize we're doing them). As you read this, have you considered abandoning the process of change before you begin? If so, let's stop that thought right here.

Instead, ask yourself a few questions: *Is fear impacting my determination? Am I afraid of success? Afraid of change?* Be honest with yourself. Fear is a major driver to self-sabotage, and by operating from a place of fear, we may reject the untapped potential we possess inside.

A few signs that you may struggle with self-sabotage include:

- Procrastinating, perhaps not engaging in taking necessary action until forced to hurry
- Being easily distracted and struggling to complete tasks
- Making excuses
- Engaging in negative self-talk, downplaying your value or ability to succeed
- Isolating or abandoning otherwise-healthy relationships

As you work through the exercises, be mindful of self-sabotaging your progress. It can help to incorporate an accountability partner. Some of these exercises will encourage you to communicate with a loved one or friend, so consider asking this trusted individual to hold you accountable for your goals of improving your self-esteem.

If you would rather keep your journey personal, you can create a visual reminder of your intentions, such as personal affirmations or a vision board, reminding you of your goals and worth.

Place these reminders where you'll see them often, such as on your phone, computer, or wall. Here, I'll write the first affirmation for you: *I am enough!*

PERFECTIONISM

Do you constantly tell yourself that you should be better or do better? If so, you may struggle with perfectionism. Perfectionism is linked to imposter syndrome, and both are rooted in fear. Striving for perfection is often caused by self-doubt and low self-esteem. A perfectionist establishes extreme standards for themselves and strives to always perform at their best, oftentimes blaming themselves for mistakes. Living with a perfectionist mindset can hinder personal growth and negatively impact relationships.

A few signs that you might struggle with perfectionism include:

- Experiencing guilt when you don't perform to your own high standards
- Feeling unwilling to ask for help and guilt and shame when others help; preferring to complete tasks alone
- Placing a high value on independence and self-sufficiency for yourself and others

- Setting unrealistic or unattainable goals but striving to achieve these goals no matter the cost
- Feeling overwhelmed and anxious trying to meet deadlines

Perfectionism can make it challenging to master new skills. You may find yourself taking more time than expected to complete these exercises because you want to do them perfectly. I can only imagine your next step in the process would be to criticize yourself as you experience guilt, but if this is you, guess what? You don't have to be perfect. I invite you to release yourself from the pressure of perfectionism, starting with this deck.

You may ask yourself, *How?* One way to release yourself from perfectionism is to practice acceptance. Focus on accepting yourself, flaws and all. Do it often, and definitely do it as you work on your self-esteem. Accept that no one is perfect, that you are trying to change, and that true, long-lasting change does not happen overnight. Give yourself grace as you proceed along your journey to greater self-esteem.

ALL-OR-NOTHING THINKING

All-or-nothing thinking forces us to see life in extremes. Our thoughts are black or white, leaving no room for middle ground. This may look like internalized thoughts such as, *I'm always messing up* or *I forgot my friend's birthday. I'm a horrible friend, and this is why no one likes me.* When we operate from this mindset, we develop a distorted sense of reality and limit ourselves from recognizing the possibilities of different ways of living and thinking.

If you can relate, let's look at some possible roots. Did you grow up in a household with strict rules? Were you criticized or shamed for not being perfect? Maybe you developed all-or-nothing thinking to understand traumatic experiences in your life? Sometimes, when we cope alone, we begin to develop unhealthy thinking patterns, which we internalize as our truths. The danger in this thought pattern is that we don't allow space to dispel these untruths or allow for new truths to enter our lives.

A few signs of all-or-nothing thinking include:

- Using words such as "always" or "never"
- Viewing life, or even simple moments, as either good or bad

- Struggling to accept any feedback as a means to learn or improve and, instead, seeing all feedback as criticism
- Ruminating on negative thoughts and catastrophizing, always thinking of the worst possible scenario or outcome
- Struggling with perfectionism

As you use the self-esteem deck, be mindful if you notice this thought pattern. Fact-check your thoughts. Are they true, or are they just your mind's perception? Several exercises will challenge your automatic thoughts, which can be a helpful first step to learning how to flip the coin and begin to operate from a more positive mindset.

PEOPLE-PLEASING

People-pleasing can hinder our willingness to change. When we have historically placed the needs of others before our own, we may hesitate to change if the change we seek might disrupt our relationships. Have you ever tried to implement a boundary with someone who violated or disregarded your rights or personal space, only to change your mind about the boundary because the individual showed anger or disappointment toward you? Or disregarded your own boundaries by saying yes to something you really didn't want to do? If this seems to be a regular occurrence for you, you may struggle with people-pleasing.

A few signs that you might have people-pleasing tendencies include:

- Fearing the negative consequences—such as guilt, disappointment, anger, etc.—of choosing your wants and needs when others make requests of you.
- Failing to celebrate yourself, even for great accomplishments, and considering this self-deprecating behavior as a necessary act of being humble
- Fearing rejection if you fail to meet the needs of others
- Being described as extremely easygoing and agreeable
- Allowing others to dictate conversation while you fail to express your perspectives, wants, or needs

Exercises within the deck will help you address this internal block. If you're nodding your head to this tendency, you may find some of the exercises challenging because they feel unnatural to your learned way of being. Don't get discouraged. There's no need to prove anything to anyone but yourself. This self-esteem deck will challenge you to establish healthy boundaries with yourself and others, and as you do, you'll learn just how to navigate from being a people-pleaser to operating from a place of self-worth and freedom to choose what's best for you.

100 Skills Cards

This deck includes 100 skills divided into six categories. Each skill will encourage you to reflect and step into empowerment in some way. Let's define the categories, how they affect self-esteem, and how the specific exercises can help:

Self-Awareness: This involves the ability to understand and recognize your own thoughts, emotions, and behaviors and how they impact yourself and others. Self-awareness also includes being able to intuit how others see you.

Without good self-awareness, we may struggle to identify our triggers and responses, which can ultimately lead to a negative view of self. A strong sense of self-awareness can boost decision-making, confidence, creativity, and more.

Self-Acceptance: This involves the ability to accept all parts of yourself, including your strengths, weaknesses, successes, and failures.

Focusing on our flaws instead of acknowledging our strengths can lead to thoughts that we aren't good enough. The self-acceptance exercises will challenge you to practice forgiveness and grace with yourself and release the expectations or opinions of others.

Self-Assertiveness: This is the ability to express oneself in a calm and confident manner, without being aggressive or passive.

Low self-esteem can result in loneliness or feeling misunderstood. If you struggle in this area, it's possible that you suffer in silence while others assume you are simply easygoing. There may also have been times when you've grown tired of being silent and lashed out with anger and aggression. This section will ask you to reflect on and challenge your communication style. You will build the ability to speak up for what you want, need, and believe in.

Self-Esteem and Purpose: This is the reason something exists.

Do you ever question your purpose in life? This section will empower you to identify your values and purpose. As you navigate this area, you may find yourself not only dreaming of who you can be but also feeling empowered to take action to live a life full of passion and fulfillment.

Self-Esteem and Core Beliefs: These are our deeply held assumptions about the world, others, and ourselves that shape our reality and behaviors.

Our core beliefs define our values and drive our decision-making, shaping our view of self and others. This section will invite you to consider when and how you established the beliefs you hold dear and to challenge, renew, or change your core beliefs going forward.

Self-Esteem and Boundaries: These are physical and emotional limits that define acceptable behavior between people. Boundaries are expectations we establish to keep us and others safe.

It's not always easy to set boundaries when self-esteem is low. This section will show you how to identify where your need for boundaries exists and learn to create healthy boundaries with yourself and others.

Resources

BOOKS

Good Boundaries and Goodbyes: Loving Others without Losing the Best of Who You Are by Lysa TerKeurst

The Mountain Is You: Transforming Self-Sabotage into Self-Mastery by Brianna Wiest

Set Boundaries, Find Peace: A Guide to Reclaiming Yourself by Nedra Glover Tawwab

The Six Pillars of Self-Esteem by Nathaniel Branden

What Happened to You? Conversations on Trauma, Resilience, and Healing by Bruce D. Perry and Oprah Winfrey

PODCAST

The Mel Robbins Podcast episode "2 Ways to Believe in Yourself & Achieve Cool Things," January 29, 2024

Index of Skills by Category

SELF-ESTEEM & PURPOSE

SELF-ESTEEM & CORE BELIEFS

SELF-ESTEEM & BOUNDARIES

About the Author

 **Dr. Leslie Davis** is an award-winning licensed clinical professional counselor specializing as a relationship therapist in Illinois and Missouri. Through her brand SHE Matters, she empowers single moms around the world to develop healthy relationships with the goal of reducing anxiety, depression, and suicidal thoughts.

An international bestselling author, she is a proud co-author of *Voices of Women: Creating Ripples of Brilliance*. Dr. Davis is also a heart mom to an amazing heart warrior son and has had the honor of providing mental health support to other heart moms in her community. When she's not facilitating healing for broken-hearted women, Dr. Davis enjoys empowering women in her community as a women's coach at 10th Planet Jiu Jitsu in O'Fallon, Illinois. Learn more about Dr. Leslie Davis by visiting therealdrleslie.com.

Zeitgeist™
An imprint and division of Penguin Random House LLC
1745 Broadway, New York, NY 10019
zeitgeistpublishing.com
penguinrandomhouse.com

Manufactured in China
First Printing

Art © by Shutterstock.com/Sylfida
Design by Katy Brown
Author photograph © by Sherah Brickell of Sherah Renee Photography
Edited by Sarah Curley

The authorized representative in the EU for product safety and compliance
is Penguin Random House Ireland, Morrison Chambers, 32 Nassau Street,
Dublin D02 YH68, Ireland. https://eu-contact.penguin.ie.